How Do You Burp in Space?

And Other Tips Every Space
Tourist Needs to Know

By Susan E. Goodman

This book belongs to : _Michael Connors_

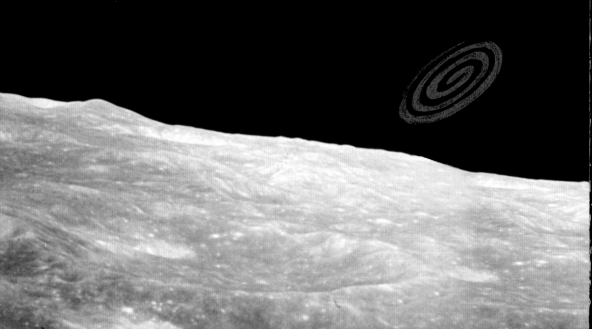

ALSO BY SUSAN E. GOODMAN

*See How They Run:
Campaign Dreams, Election Schemes,
and the Race to the White House*

ALSO ILLUSTRATED BY MICHAEL SLACK

Scapegoat

How Do You BURP in Space?

And Other Tips Every Space Tourist Needs to Know

SUSAN E. GOODMAN

iLLUSTRATED BY MICHAEL SLACK

BLOOMSBURY
NEW YORK   LONDON   NEW DELHI   SYDNEY

First published in the United States of America in July 2013
by Bloomsbury Children's Books
www.bloomsbury.com

For information about permission to reproduce selections from this book, write to
Permissions, Bloomsbury Children's Books, 175 Fifth Avenue, New York, New York 10010
Bloomsbury books may be purchased for business or promotional use. For information
on bulk purchases please contact Macmillan Corporate and Premium Sales Department at
specialmarkets@macmillan.com

Spaceport image on page 3 copyright © Foster + Partners
All other images copyright © NASA/courtesy of nasaimages.org

Library of Congress Cataloging-in-Publication Data
Goodman, Susan E.
How do you burp in space? : and other tips every space tourist needs to know /
by Susan E. Goodman ; illustrated by Michael Slack. — 1st U.S. ed.
p.   cm.
Summary: A nonfiction travel guide to space tourism that includes
information about accommodations, attractions, and more.
ISBN 978-1-59990-068-1 (hardcover) • ISBN 978-1-59990-934-9 (reinforced)
1. Manned space flight—Juvenile literature. 2. Interplanetary voyages—Juvenile literature.
3. Space tourism—Juvenile literature. I. Slack, Michael H., ill. II. Title
TL793.G645 2013   629.45—dc23   2011035303

Printed in China by Toppan Leefung Printers, Ltd., Dongguan, Guangdong
2 4 6 8 10 9 7 5 3 1 (hardcover)
2 4 6 8 10 9 7 5 3 1 (reinforced)

All papers used by Bloomsbury Publishing, Inc., are natural, recyclable products
made from wood grown in well-managed forests. The manufacturing processes
conform to the environmental regulations of the country of origin.

To Alyssa Casden—one of my favorite fellow travelers
—S. E. G.

To Ham—without you we would never have reached the stars
—M. S.

CONTENTS

INTRODUCTION

A VACATION THAT'S "OUT OF THIS WORLD"

No doubt about it: the day is coming. A few tourists have been up there already. Private companies are testing their ships. If you go to New Mexico (or online), you can visit Spaceport America, the world's first spaceport built especially for tourist launches and other commercial space travel.

It may not be this year or next, but soon ordinary people like you will be blasting into space. The first flights will be short, just high enough above Earth that you can float around the cabin and look down on that blue-and-green ball we call home. But don't forget your camera! You'll have plenty of time to take pictures.

SPACE STORIES
The next time I go into space, I'll be able to take my family with me.
—ASTRONAUT KATHRYN THORNTON

Eventually, you'll be able to orbit Earth or vacation on the Moon. It's too early to make reservations, but it's never too soon to start thinking about it. This guidebook will help you enjoy your space adventure long before you board the ship. After all, how can you daydream about it without knowing what you'll eat and where you'll sleep? Or what it's like doing any of this while floating upside down?

SPACE STORIES

It goes well beyond anything that I have ever dreamed. Living in space is like having a different life, living in a different world.

—DENNIS TITO, FIRST SPACE TOURIST, 2001

A visualization of Spaceport America

1

PLANNING YOUR TRIP

WHAT TO PACK

What can you take into space? Not much. Ships don't have room for extras. Typically each US astronaut can bring only two pounds of personal items. Luckily clothes and toothbrushes are provided by the US space agency, NASA (National Aeronautics and Space Administration). Still, two pounds isn't much when you realize that this guidebook weighs almost a pound. If you want a stuffed animal for bedtime, bring a small one. A picture of your family? Leave the frame at home.

Perhaps you're thinking, "I should be able to bring more because everything in space is weightless, anyhow." Nice try, but that argument doesn't work. Between the price of fuel and everything else, it used to cost about $10,000 for the shuttle to carry each pound of weight into orbit. That makes the candy you wanted to sneak aboard pretty expensive.

DON'T WASTE THE WEIGHT

You don't need the following items in space. Why? Just think about it. If you can't figure it out, keep reading. Actually, keep reading anyway!

★ cell phone

★ flip-flops

★ bubble bath

★ postcards

★ pogo stick

★ spray deodorant

★ skirts

★ juggling balls

CLOTHING

No matter who supplies them, you'll wear comfortable clothes on board: short- or long-sleeved shirts, and special pants covered with pockets and Velcro so you can "stick or store" things that would otherwise drift away. For space walks, you'll need an entirely different outfit (more about that later).

Space travelers wear only socks around the ship to keep their feet warm. Why would you need shoes to float around? The only time you will wear shoes is when you're on the treadmill (more about this later, too).

TOURIST TIP

If you wear glasses, bring a strap. Otherwise, when you move your head too quickly, they could fly off and float away.

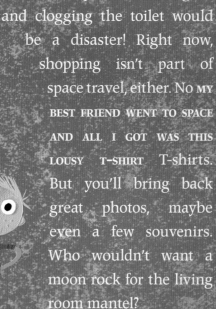

MONEY

This is a pay-before-you-go vacation. No bringing money for extras like candy in vending machines. A bunch of quarters floating off and clogging the toilet would be a disaster! Right now, shopping isn't part of space travel, either. No MY BEST FRIEND WENT TO SPACE AND ALL I GOT WAS THIS LOUSY T-SHIRT T-shirts. But you'll bring back great photos, maybe even a few souvenirs. Who wouldn't want a moon rock for the living room mantel?

SPACE SPEAK FOR TRAVELERS

When you travel to any foreign place, it's good to know some of the language. Don't worry—you won't be chatting with aliens in space (we hope!). But the astronauts who fly your ship have a whole different vocabulary. Here are some expressions to get you started.

Big Blue Marble: a nickname for Earth

bird: any spacecraft

controlled descent: a landing (as opposed to a crash)

everything's in the green: A-OK; things are going great

g's: units of gravity; three g's, for example, is a force three times the pull of Earth's gravity

go outside: space walk

the ISS: the International Space Station

Mr. Thirsty: the funnel part of a space toilet

NEO: a Near-Earth Object, such as an asteroid (NEO is pronounced "nee-oh," although astronauts may be thinking, "Oh no!")

nominal: very good

off-scale high: off the charts; the needle of a cockpit instrument passing its highest reading or someone's excitement about seeing something wonderful

Snoopy cap: the fabric cap containing earphones and a microphone worn under a space suit so you can talk to people in your ship and back on Earth

space junk: orbiting rocket parts and other human-made trash

Astronaut Bernard A. Harris Jr.

THE BEST TIME TO GO

Tourists pick sunny seasons for beach vacations and snowy ones for skiing. Just about any time works in space, though. There's no hurricane season in space. No rainy season, either—in fact, no rain at all.

The universe does have its own brand of bad weather, from solar radiation storms and geomagnetic storms to the occasional galactic ray. Luckily, the US National Weather Service tracks what's going on up there. They even issue space-storm warnings. So, you'll know when to cancel a space walk and stay inside the ship.

Otherwise, space weather doesn't change much. The temperature basically depends upon how close you are to a star like our Sun and whether you're in light or shadow. Average temperature near the International Space Station: 250 degrees Fahrenheit in the light—heat that could easily boil water, and you, too, if you were unprotected. Then the temperature drops to 250 degrees below zero in the shade, colder than the coldest spot on Earth. If you think that's chilly, get ready for 387 degrees below zero on the far side of the Moon!

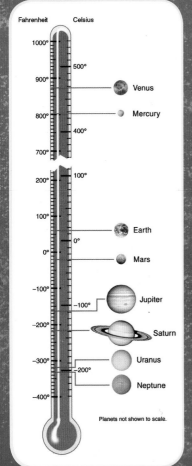

Fahrenheit Celsius

1000°
         500°
900°
                Venus
800°   Mercury
         400°

700°

         100°
200°

100°

                Earth
0°   0°
                Mars

-100°
         -100° Jupiter

-200°
                Saturn

-300°   Uranus
         -200°
                Neptune
-400°

Planets not shown to scale.

HEALTH ISSUES

Tourists must take physical exams to make sure they're healthy enough for space travel. People with heart problems shouldn't go; the strain of takeoff and reentry could be dangerous. People with contagious diseases must wait until they won't infect other passengers. Anyone in a cast must wait, too; broken bones might not mend well in microgravity. Don't worry about bumps and scratches once you're there. Cuts form scabs and heal just fine.

A crew member is trained in first aid, but there aren't any medical centers in space. So stay healthy. Doctors on Earth could radio your "space doc" with medical advice, but even emergency operations aren't a good idea. In microgravity, *everything* floats around and no one may know exactly where your appendix is!

ⓘ TRAVEL ALERT: TEARDROPS DON'T DROP!

CRYING IN SPACE is so weird, you just might forget why you're doing it. Tears well up and cling to your eyes, creating a bigger and bigger ball until you move them away. Gravity is what pulls them down your cheeks.

While working outside the bird, Astronaut David A. Wolf has a great view of the Big Blue Marble!

2
GETTING THERE

GOING UP

How *are* you going to get into space? Good question. Several countries are working on new vehicles. Private space tourism companies are, too. So we can't give you an exact description of your ship, but we do know it will travel *up*—and *fast!*

If it's like the shuttle, your ship will hitch a ride on rocket boosters. Fasten your safety belt—the rockets fire and *bam!* Four seconds later you're racing at 100 miles an hour. In forty seconds, you're zooming faster than the speed of sound. The boosters fall away. The clouds shrink to points of white. The sky fades from blue to black. In about eight minutes, you're 155 miles above Earth, at least 145 miles higher than you'd be in a regular plane. That's high enough to go into orbit.

Some space tourism companies are working on other ideas: one is sending a huge airplane high into the atmosphere. Then it releases a smaller space plane, which quickly fires its own rocket booster, taking its passengers toward the stars three times faster than the speed of sound.

PREFLIGHT TRAINING

Astronauts train for years to go on their missions and so will your flight crew. As a tourist, your preparation will be much shorter. Your training teaches you what happens during each part of the trip and what you need to know how to do.

You'll also learn how to deal with g-force. Big objects, like planets, have a lot of gravity, which pulls all objects to them. As ships leave and return to Earth's atmosphere, travelers are pressed down into their seats for a few moments. That's g-force at work. Astronauts have described g-force as a giant hand pushing against you and compared it to being sat on by a three-hundred-pound gorilla.

This pressure makes it feel hard to breathe, so you learn to push your lips together, then inhale and exhale very slowly. Simulators on Earth create the g-force so you can practice. You can also practice tightening your arm and leg muscles to keep your blood flowing. Sounds a little scary, but practice makes perfect!

How do you practice working in *heavy* space suits while in Earth's gravity? Astronauts such as Heidemarie M. Stefanyshyn-Piper, pictured here, train in NASA's Neutral Buoyancy Lab (a GIANT swimming pool), large enough to hold full-size models of the International Space Station's modules.

SPACE STORIES

Yoweee! . . .
I've never felt so free.
—ASTRONAUT DEKE SLAYTON

WELCOME TO SPACE

G-force can be trying but, suddenly, about fifty miles above Earth, that three-hundred-pound gorilla is gone. You no longer feel or hear the ship's movement. You're still strapped into your seat, but you're floating against the harness. You let go of this guidebook and it hovers in midair. The hair of the person next to you is drifting outward.

You're weightless!

We don't know who will actually be sitting near you, but this crazy hairdo belongs to astronaut Marsha Ivins.

TRAVEL ALERT: THE LOWDOWN ON GRAVITY: BEFORE YOU GO ANYWHERE, LET'S CLEAR UP THIS ZERO-GRAVITY BUSINESS

ZERO G'S IN SPACE? *Wrong!* If there were no gravity in space, stars and planets would be drifting all over the place instead of neatly staying in their orbits. In other words, there are g's everywhere—lots of them. So scientists now use the word "microgravity" instead of "zero g's" to describe the fact that everything floats up there.

Sadly, even the word "microgravity" is misleading. When astronauts are floating around in orbit, they are still being pulled toward Earth by 97 percent of its gravity. What's so "micro" about that? Nothing. *What is going on?*

If you want to understand this weighty puzzle (and what self-respecting space tourist wouldn't?), turn to page 57 for a complete explanation. Meanwhile, trust your guidebook—even if you don't feel it, gravity is everywhere!

Astronaut Stephanie Wilson floats middeck of the space shuttle *Discovery*.

3
GETTING ORIENTED

RESET YOUR WATCHES!

On Earth we set our clocks using local time zones. When a boy goes to bed at 9:00 p.m. Eastern time in New York, a girl in Los Angeles is just sitting down to her dinner at 6:00 Pacific time. Using this system in space would be crazy. While orbiting Earth, you pass through a time zone about every four minutes. So NASA uses MET (Mission Elapsed Time). At launch, the clock starts at 00:00:00:00. The two zeros on the far left measure days, the next two count hours, the next two count minutes, and the last two count seconds. When it's 01:06:31:56 MET, you are 1 day, 6 hours, 31 minutes, and 56 seconds into your fabulous vacation.

- DAYS
- HOURS
- MINUTES
- SECONDS

No matter what time it is, you've got to let your folks know you've arrived safely. Most travel guides supply area codes for phone calls in your new location. Not this one! Can you imagine good cell reception on the Moon? Or the roaming charges? In space, you contact friends and family with e-mail or by webcam. The International Space Station, for example, has a high-speed antenna that gives it Internet service whenever the station (and the antenna!) is in position to get the connection. Astronauts surf the Web by using a laptop on board to control a computer on Earth.

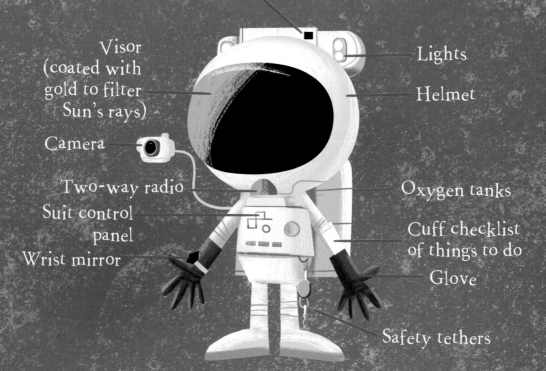

TV camera

Lights

Visor
(coated with
gold to filter
Sun's rays)

Helmet

Camera

Two-way radio

Oxygen tanks

Suit control
panel

Cuff checklist
of things to do

Wrist mirror

Glove

Safety tethers

Space walks are great photo opportunities!

GETTING AROUND

Most travel guides tell you how to get around your destination by car, subway, or even bicycle. In space, you've got your ship—that's all.

Actually, that's not true. You also have a space suit, which is like a personal spaceship, if you think about it. A space suit lets you go outside to explore. Scientists are already making updated models.

No matter what suit you wear, it's a thrill to ease through that open hatch. You pull gently on the exterior handrail and you're outside!

Cables keep you safely attached to the ship, but you feel free. You're whizzing around Earth at five miles per second. Yet you feel motionless. It seems as if it's the planet that's moving.

SPACE STORIES

All right. I'll open the door and come through . . .
It's the saddest moment of my life.
—ASTRONAUT EDWARD WHITE,
ENDING AMERICA'S FIRST SPACE WALK

If you can take your eyes off Earth, there's plenty to see. You're a human satellite with the universe all around you. Watch star fields drift overhead. Find your favorite constellations. Create your own.

Most space walks are shorter than six hours, but your suit lets you stay out for seven or more hours. If you get hungry, turn your head and munch on an energy bar Velcro-ed near one shoulder. Thirsty? A water pouch with a straw is near the other.

TRAVEL ALERT:

LEAVING THE SHIP is complicated, so you can't duck back in to use the bathroom. Instead, you wear something that's called a Maximum Absorption Garment. (Yes, it's a lot like a diaper!) Just call it a MAG for short and think of it as a pair of disposable underpants.

DEALING WITH WEIGHTLESSNESS

Most beginners try to move around the ship by swimming. Hey, you're not in water, you're in space! Getting where you want to go is easy, but it takes practice. Push or pull against something to aim your body in the right direction. Just one flick of your finger or foot will do. Otherwise, you'll crash into the other side of the cabin.

Weightlessness (microgravity) is exciting. But remember, everything floats, not just you, which makes things complicated. Imagine preparing a hot dog. Split the bun, then trade the knife for a fork to spear the frankfurter. Oops—the knife is floating away. You grab it and end up holding the knife and bun in one hand and the forked frankfurter in the other. Even after you get the meat in the bun, how will you open the relish? See the problem? (To learn about what you'll be eating and how, turn to our dining section on page 35.)

Microgravity also affects your body. The good news? You grow taller because gravity isn't pushing the bones of your spine as close together. The bad news? You'll look a little weird. The fluids in your body shift upward rather than being pulled low by Earth's gravity. So your legs get skinny. In fact, people call them the "chicken legs" of space. Some of the fluid travels up toward your head, so you get a puffy face, too. You may also feel stuffed up, like you have a cold.

That's not why you'll be sneezing so much, though. Dust floats around the ship in microgravity instead of settling on the ground like normal.

WARNING: Sneezes float, too. Make sure you have tissues handy!

EXERCISE

If you're in space for a week or more, you need to add exercise to your daily schedule. On Earth, you exercise even when you're standing still. Gravity pushes you down and your body works against it to stand straight and tall. In space, your muscles and bones don't have any work to do. They start getting weaker right away. So you've got to help them.

Lifting weights in weightlessness isn't the answer! You harness yourself to a treadmill that presses you down so you feel like you're moving in gravity. Those straps can rub against your skin and make it sore, especially if you're jogging for a long time. The sweat that balls up on your body can be annoying, too (remember, it doesn't drip down without gravity).

Sometimes, however, it's worth it. In 2007 astronaut Suni Williams signed up for the Boston Marathon but couldn't get home in time. She ran it in space instead, starting at the same moment as everyone else on Earth. After four hours, twenty-three minutes, and forty-six seconds, she finished the 26.2-mile race. That's pretty fast. Meanwhile, her ship did a lot better. It circled the planet almost three times.

SPACE STORIES

The treadmill is a little tough. The first time I got on there, I couldn't even do a mile and my legs were wobbling back and forth."
—ASTRONAUT SUNITA WILLIAMS

During the marathon, astronaut Suni Williams ran a speed of about six miles per hour, while the shuttle flew more than five miles per second.

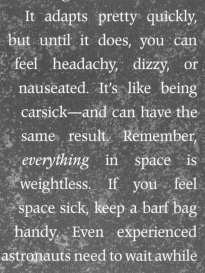

SPACE SICKNESS

Sadly, you pay a price for being a space tourist—besides the cost of your ticket. Most people get a bit queasy at first. The problem is that you don't *feel* any different when you're floating right side up, upside down, or sideways, because you don't feel the pull of gravity. But you *see* yourself in these odd positions and your brain gets confused.

It adapts pretty quickly, but until it does, you can feel headachy, dizzy, or nauseated. It's like being carsick—and can have the same result. Remember, *everything* in space is weightless. If you feel space sick, keep a barf bag handy. Even experienced astronauts need to wait awhile before doing their "Yeah, space!" flips and rolls. Most travelers feel better within a few days or take medicine to adjust even faster.

MAPS

As you're learning your way around weightlessness, learn your way around the universe, too. Here is a map of our solar system so you'll know where you're going (and where you wish you were going!).

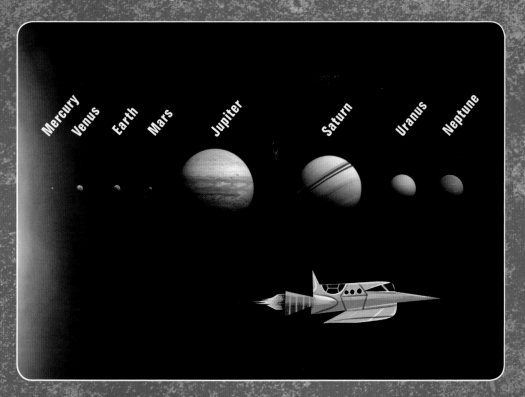

Mercury Venus Earth Mars Jupiter Saturn Uranus Neptune

SPACE STORIES

If I had a nickel for every time I said "incredible" during a space flight, I'd have enough savings to pay my way back as a tourist.

—ASTRONAUT TOM JONES

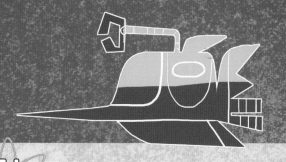

4

ACCOMMODATIONS

The International Space Station has welcomed a few tourists, but it was really built for astronauts and scientists. Someday a company will build an orbiting hotel for travelers, instead. Eventually, someone will also build a resort on the Moon.

Until then, tourists will see the sights from the comfort of their ship. Think of it as a space cruise. Life on a spaceship is half the adventure.

BEDROOMS

Space is hard to come by in space, so your bedroom will be quite small. It will probably have a light, an air vent, and a sliding door to give you some privacy—not a lot more. It may not be much larger than the lower bunk of a bunk bed.

That's okay. You won't need much room. There won't be a bed. Microgravity is one giant air mattress. Don't expect a blanket. Even the heaviest one would just float away.

You don't "lie down" either. Some astronauts zip themselves into sleeping bags with one rigid side so they feel like they're actually lying on something. Most use a thinner bag and attach it to the wall so they don't float around. A pillow is more trouble than it's worth—you have to strap it on to your head with Velcro.

Do you curl up in a ball when you sleep? Sorry, that's a problem, too. In space, you can't really sleep on your side or stomach. Horizontal, vertical, upside down—they are all the same! No matter what position you're in when you fall asleep, you turn into a snoozing Frankenstein. Once you relax, your arms drift out in front of you.

TOURIST TIP

Don't ask for a room with a view. In space, sleep time and nighttime aren't the same thing. A ship orbits Earth every ninety minutes, which means you get a mini-version of day and night every ninety minutes, too. To avoid the light, most astronauts wear what they call a Lone Ranger mask.

BATHROOMS

Keeping clean

Between microgravity and conserving your precious water supply, keeping clean in space can be tricky. For example:

✦ You must keep your lips firmly closed while brushing your teeth to avoid foamy glop floating around the cabin. Since normal sinks need gravity to work, rinsing is

Astronauts Frank Culbertson and Daniel Bursch

a problem. Astronauts use edible toothpaste and just swallow it when they're finished.

✦ Do you like long, hot showers? Then enjoy one before your trip! Years ago, some spacecrafts had showers. Taking them *was* long (about an hour and a half), but not much fun. In space, water is weightless like everything else. Imagine trying to herd the droplets onto your body. Once there, the water sticks to you so you must vacuum it off! On your trip, you'll wash yourself with a wet towel and special soap that doesn't need to be rinsed.

✦ You will also have no-rinse shampoo for your hair. Brushing helps with

tangles, but forget your normal hairdo. Create a floating space-do instead, because that's what you're going to get. If your hair's long, it might even form a bubble around your head.

Astronaut Tracy Caldwell Dyson

✦ Once you're clean, apply lots of lotion because it's very dry in spaceships. Astronauts do and they *still* shed twice as many skin cells as they would on Earth. Imagine that drifting cloud of old skin if the ship wasn't filtering its air.

Space toilets

Learning to use a space toilet can take some getting used to. Don't get discouraged, though. Potty training was harder—and you figured that one out when you were a little kid. Toilets on Earth rely on gravity, so water—and everything else—flushes down and away. As you know by now, there is no "down" in space. So you pee into something that looks like a funnel—if you have read "Space Speak for Travelers," page 8, you'll know its nickname! A gentle vacuum draws the pee through a tube into a collecting tank.

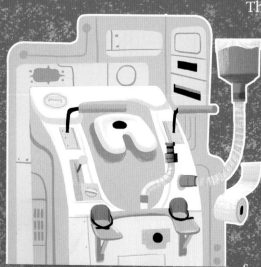

The same type of vacuum sucks poop into the toilet's other tank. No funnel for that kind of bathroom visit, thank goodness. Instead, you sit on the toilet and keep yourself there by sliding bars across your thighs. Otherwise, you'd float away—and that could make an awful mess.

If this space toilet seems too nerve-racking, you can always wait for resorts on the Moon or Mars. The Moon has one-sixth of Earth's gravity and Mars has about one-third, so things *can* flow downward. These hotels will have more user-friendly bathrooms.

SPACE IS "GREEN"

In space, you recycle almost everything. People always need clean air to breathe (and they can't get a new supply by opening the window!). So the air is filtered and reused. Your ship may

also have plants on board because they clean the air of carbon dioxide that we don't need and release the oxygen that we do.

On longer trips, water also needs to be recycled. It is gathered from everywhere. It is collected from the steam, sweat, and exhaled breath that's in the air. It's also recovered from washing, the ship's fuel cells, and, yes, even urine.

If you're a little grossed out, tell yourself that this water, once purified, is much cleaner than the stuff you drink at home. Or remember that you're taking the trip of your dreams, even if drinking your sweat and pee sounds like a nightmare. Being an explorer requires some sacrifice!

TOURIST TIP

Do not pack any lotions or sanitizers made with alcohol. As you just learned, the ship recycles moisture from the air for its water supply. If this moisture included alcohol, you'd end up drinking liquor!

5

DINING

EATING IN MIDAIR

A guidebook to New York or Orlando would list good restaurant choices for every corner of town. As a pioneer of space tourism, you can't expect fly-thru burger joints and fancy restaurants.

Your ship will probably offer meals similar to the ones astronauts eat right now. It may not be the best food *in* the world, but it's the best food *out*side of it. And light-years better than the goo early astronauts squeezed out of toothpaste-like tubes—nutritious but no tastier than toothpaste itself.

Even today, there's no real cooking on board. Your space chef will mostly reheat prepared foods stored in pouches. To save room and weight, foods like mac and cheese or scrambled eggs are dehydrated. Before serving, the chef mixes hot water back in. Other treats, such as brownies, granola bars, and fruit cocktail, can be eaten right out of the package.

Astronaut Clayton Anderson

No dinner table on ship. No chairs, either. You strap a tray to your thigh and float through lunch with friends. The tray has Velcro or slots to anchor your food cartons. Your silverware is magnetized so it sticks to the tray. You also have a pair of scissors to cut open your food pouches.

Most space food is purposefully sticky so it stays on your spoon until it reaches your mouth. Then you wash it down with water, juice, or lemonade, but not from a glass.

Nothing pours in microgravity. OJ remains in a glass even if you tilt it. Straws in drink pouches

If astronaut Edward Michael "Mike" Fincke is trying to juggle in space, he should know better!

work fine as long as they have a clip. On Earth, when you're done sipping, gravity pulls any liquid left in the straw back downward. In space it keeps flowing (all over the ship!) until you clamp the straw shut.

PLAY WITH YOUR FOOD

Not supposed to play with your food at home? Come to space and . . .

+ Drink with chopsticks. Grab your juice or tea bag (in space, a tea bag is actually a bag of brewed tea). Squeeze a blob out through your straw. In microgravity, floating liquids form a ball. Play pick-up-with-sticks and quench your thirst.

+ Place a cookie in the air and "fly" a friend toward it so she can catch it in her mouth.

+ Set spoonfuls of food a-twirling and—guess what!—catch them in your mouth.

+ Play M&M'S baseball. Pitch an M&M toward a friend who uses his hand as a bat. The rest of the players field with their mouths!

+ Try Astronaut R. Mike Mullane's trick. He built a solar system using orange juice as the sun and M&M'S as the planets.

SPACE STORIES

Scrambled eggs . . . are not quite sticky enough to stay on a spoon. I quickly learned to hold the carton close to my mouth and use my spoon to aim each bite.

—ASTRONAUT SALLY RIDE

WHAT'S ON THE MENU?

Meals must pass many tests to make it on to the space menu, but there are plenty to choose from. Cornflakes, oatmeal, hot dogs, spaghetti with meatballs, and tuna or ham sandwiches are just part of the list. If you're a vegetarian, you can have peanut butter, yogurt, and dried fruit. Then there are snacks like trail mix, candy, and cookies.

Make sure to ask for extra ketchup and salsa. Remember the body fluid that drifts toward your head and makes your nose feel stuffy? When you can't smell food well, you can't taste it very well, either. Most astronauts pile on the spice.

Since you're on an adventure, try eating adventurously, too. Astronauts from different countries work on the International Space Station, and they like having their favorite foods around. Can you guess which countries added the following dishes to the space menu?

1. Dried moose meat and gingerbread cookies
2. Pork with garlic sauce, stir-fried chicken, and moon cakes
   (given where you are, who could resist those?)
3. Herring, pretzel sticks, and hot mustard
4. Roast quail in wine sauce, celery-root puree, and rice pudding with fruit
5. Seaweed soup, ramen noodles, and salmon rice balls
6. Chicken biryani, chapatis, and fruit juices
7. Pickled-cucumber–and–meat soup, beef goulash, and
   honey cake

1. Sweden 2. China 3. Germany 4. France 5. Japan 6. India 7. Russia.

SPACE-FOOD NO-NO'S

✦ **Most bread and crackers:** They have too many crumbs that could waft into machinery! Space sandwiches use flour tortillas instead.

✦ **Salt and pepper shakers:** The flakes would spice up the cabin, not your food. Salt is dissolved in water and squeezed onto food. Pepper doesn't dissolve, so it's put in vegetable oil.

✦ **Astronaut ice cream:** That stuff sold in museum shops has never been part of the space program!

✦ **Soda pop:** This deserves a section all its own . . .

WHY NO SODA IN SPACE?

The real question is: How do you burp in space? The answer? It isn't easy—or pretty. Astronauts in the 1980s found this out the hard way.

Back then, the Coca-Cola Company wanted Coke to be the first soft drink in space. It spent a fortune figuring out how to make a can of Coke that kept its bubbles, or carbonation, in microgravity.

Astronaut Anthony W. England

Astronauts quickly wished they had left that fizz back home. Carbonation makes you burp. On Earth, bubbles in soda pop are lighter than the liquid around them, so they rise to the top of your stomach and you burp them out. In space, everything is weightless, so nothing is lighter than anything else. The carbonation stays mixed with whatever else is in your stomach. That means that when you burp, it brings up the carbonation *and* all the food and liquid nearby!

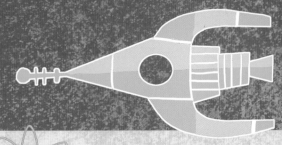

6
WHAT TO SEE AND DO

Space is so amazing, you can sightsee with your eyes closed. Or, let's say, you can see some of its sights on your eyelids! How? Galactic cosmic rays travel through space. Their particles are so tiny, they can pass right through your body. If they go through your brain, they create dazzling fireworks on your eyelids.

What else can you see and do on your trip?

FUN ON BOARD

On ship, you can watch movies, play video games, listen to music, and read—just like you do at home. But you aren't at home, so try to . . .

STARGAZE—BETTER THAN IN HOLLYWOOD

The song "Twinkle, Twinkle, Little Star" only makes sense on Earth. Stars twinkle because we look at them through our atmosphere. In space, they shine steadily and brightly in white or blue, orange or red.

A double cluster of stars in one of our neighboring galaxies puts on quite a show.

How about constellations? You can still spot them in space, but since you see so many more stars, it's harder to pick them out. Study your star map to find the Big Dipper, Orion (the hunter), and other favorites. Then search for constellations you've never seen before. Out on a space walk, you're in the biggest planetarium there is!

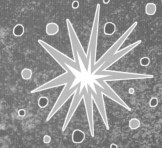

ADMIRE ONE SPECIAL STAR: OUR SUN

Our Sun has a bluish tone in space. It looks brighter, too. It won't look as bright as it is, though. The ship's windows are coated to block the Sun's ultraviolet rays. Otherwise, looking at this star would blind you.

If you like sunrises and sunsets, you're in luck. Orbiting Earth about every ninety minutes, you see each of them sixteen times every twenty-four hours. Yet it's a sight you won't grow tired of. Within just seconds, you race through at least eight bands of color, from brilliant red to the deepest blue.

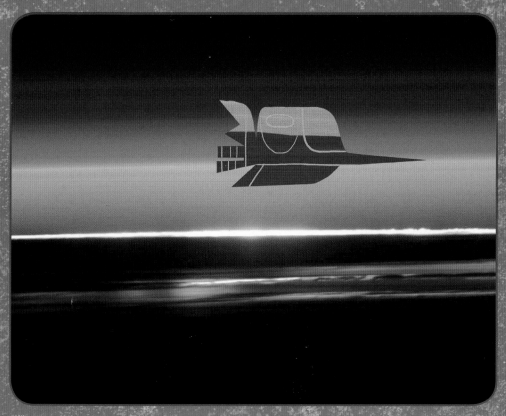

What a sunset!

EARTH-WATCH

You're out there to explore space, but oddly enough, people's favorite activity is looking back at Earth. In fact, all NASA ships carry cleaning materials to wipe nose prints off the windows. Looking up through our atmosphere makes space hard to see. Looking down doesn't cause the same problem. So . . .

• Test your geography skills by finding the United States, the mitten of Michigan, Italy's boot, and the down-under continent of Australia. Don't forget Mount Everest!

• Watch the weather: hurricanes whirling in the oceans, lightning jumping through clouds, dust storms in deserts, and raging wildfires. Keep

A volcano in Alaska

looking: there's a volcano erupting somewhere on Earth every few days.

The nighttime lights of New York City

• See cities turn into swirls of light at dusk.

• People used to think that the Great Wall of China was the only human-made structure you could see from space. Prove them wrong. Have a contest with your friends: Who can see

the smallest object down there? An airport? An airplane's vapor trail? Perhaps even people if you use a telescope.

- Keep an eye on the top and bottom of the planet. High-energy particles from the Sun collide with gases in Earth's atmosphere and glow green, red, or blue violet. Scientists call this event an aurora. You'll call it the most incredible light show you've ever seen!

SPACE STORIES

The first day or so we all pointed to our countries.
The third or fourth day we were pointing to our continents.
By the fifth day, we were aware of only one Earth.
— ASTRONAUT SULTAN BIN SALMAN BIN ABDUL AZIZ AL-SAUD

PLAY SPACE BINGO

Have you ever played bingo—trying to cover a line of numbers all the way across, down, or diagonally? Try the space version, where you check off sights you've found while looking out the window or on a space walk. The prize for seeing these marvels? Isn't seeing them prize enough?

asteroid ✦ the rings of Saturn ✦ a solar storm

Jupiter's weather belts ✦ an aurora at one of Earth's poles ✦ a comet

a satellite orbiting Earth ✦ a hurricane on Earth ✦ space junk

VISITING THE MOON

On July 20, 1969, *Apollo 11* astronaut Neil Armstrong was the first person to walk on the Moon. He was also its first tourist, if you think about it (the first human one, anyway!). Only eleven astronauts have followed him, and none since 1972.

Eventually, the Moon will be a popular vacation spot. It doesn't really take too long to get there. It's about 250,000 miles away, but a spaceship can get there in three days.

LAST STOP BEFORE THE MOON

GALAXY BURGER

WHERE TO STAY

If you go before the first resorts are built, you'll sleep on your orbiting ship and take a space taxi down to the surface for day trips. If you wait long enough, however, hotels will be built that can deal with the Moon's extreme temperatures and block the Sun's ultraviolet rays. Imagine what architects will create: structures impossible to build on Earth will soar in the Moon's low gravity. And think how much you'll enjoy the shower and flush toilets after three days on the ship!

WHAT TO SEE AND DO

Play in one-sixth gravity

The Moon has gravity, but less than Earth because it's smaller. Walking on it takes practice. You lope instead of stroll and often have both feet off the ground at the same time. You must plan ahead when you want to stop or turn.

Low gravity lets you jump higher than on Earth. You can hurdle over a friend in a game of lunar leapfrog. You can play golf, if you don't mind losing the ball. When astronaut Alan B. Shepard Jr. gave it a try, his ball sailed out of sight. Maybe some version of paintball would be better. You could bounce out of range and hide in craters.

Staff from your ship or hotel can take you to places where these activities are allowed. Once tourism on the Moon begins, vast areas will be restricted to preserve the Moon's natural beauty. As you'll soon learn, footprint pollution will be a problem.

Visit historical sites

Learn about the daring Apollo space program that landed a man on the Moon. Visit parts of ships and moon buggies left behind. You can also still see astronauts' footprints that were pressed into lunar dust so long ago. There is no wind on the Moon to blow them away.

Other highlights: US flags and plaques to commemorate six landings; a gold olive branch to symbolize peace, left by Neil Armstrong; cast-off space suits; and the statue *Fallen Astronaut*, which honors the astronauts and cosmonauts who have lost their lives exploring space.

Ride a moon buggy

Lunar rovers, or moon buggies, don't go too fast and it's just as well. Driving on moondust is slippery, like riding on snow. There won't be many roads on the Moon, so you'll have to be careful. If you launch your buggy off a hill, it will fly pretty far before one-sixth gravity brings it down again!

This lunar rover has been on the Moon since 1971.

Explore

Jump into a crater. Collect rocks. Visit one of the Moon's mountain ranges. Decide if you agree with Neil Armstrong that the Moon smells like wet ashes. Sign your name in the dust, but use your best handwriting. It might last forever.

Play indoors

Inside a hotel or Moon gym, you can take off your space suit and enjoy everything one-sixth gravity has to offer. Dunk a basketball? No problem. It's a great place to practice gymnastics, although trampolines might be dangerous.

Why not try something totally new? Strap on some wings and start flapping. You should be able to fly across the room.

TRAVEL ALERT:

CLOSE ENCOUNTERS? EXPERTS have no proof that aliens exist. Most think they do, given all the planets in the universe. The idea of meeting one is exciting, but it's more likely to be a tiny bacteria-like organism than ET. If you do have a "close encounter," don't get too close. You wouldn't want to catch an extraterrestrial disease. When asked how he would have handled an alien, astronaut R. Mike Mullane said, "I would have grabbed the microphone and called, 'Houston, we have a problem.'"

KNOCK KNOCK

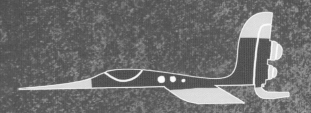

7
GOING HOME

REENTRY

You may want to stay in space forever, but sooner or later you'll be on your way home. How you return depends upon your ship. Most spacecrafts' engines work only in space. Once back in Earth's atmosphere, the crafts simply glide to a landing strip. Many early tourist flights may well do the same.

If you are riding a ship like the shuttle, as you get closer to Earth you'll start to notice wisps of atmosphere whipping past your window. The friction of reentry heats the surrounding air into your last spectacular light show. As the temperature climbs, an eerie white glow turns red, then orange, until a huge pink flame bathes the ship. You've become a cotton-candy-pink comet with a fiery tail of white, yellow, and purple light.

All at once, your time in microgravity is over. Your body jams back into its seat. A storm

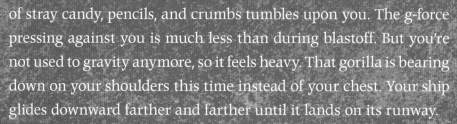

of stray candy, pencils, and crumbs tumbles upon you. The g-force pressing against you is much less than during blastoff. But you're not used to gravity anymore, so it feels heavy. That gorilla is bearing down on your shoulders this time instead of your chest. Your ship glides downward farther and farther until it lands on its runway.

Welcome back to Earth!

GETTING USED TO GRAVITY

You may be happy to get home, but you won't be jumping for joy. After living in microgravity, your arms and head feel like weights. Even standing up is hard work. Your heart beats faster as it gets used to pushing blood "up" again.

They may be smiling for the camera, but these adventurers know that walking to the terminal will be tough. From left to right: Astronauts Kenneth Ham, Karen Nyberg, Akihiko Hoshide, Mark Kelly, Michael Fossum, and Ronald Garan

You may also feel a little dizzy. Your body reduced its blood supply in space because you don't need as much of it there. Drink lots of liquids and the feeling will go away pretty soon.

It's hard to walk in gravity at first. Some travelers say those first steps feel like you're wearing cement shoes. Others say your sense of balance will be unsteady. Hold on to the railing when you leave the ship. Unused muscles weaken fast, but they get strong fast, too. It takes anywhere from a day to a week to feel normal again.

SPACE STORIES

After floating in space for 2 weeks, I felt like I weighed 2,000 pounds when I landed back on Earth. My feet felt so heavy and hard to lift—as if they were stuck in some chewing gum on the floor.

—ASTRONAUT DON THOMAS

LONG-TERM EFFECTS OF SPACE TRAVEL

Spending a long time in space will definitely affect your body. That's why scientists need to figure out how to keep us healthy when we travel to Mars. Don't worry, short jaunts in space don't have long-term effects on your health.

Yet there's no question, space travel will change your life. After all, how many other kids will be able to say, "I've been in space and it's out of this world"? You may find it also changes the way you see the world. As astronaut Ken Bowersox says, "You don't see any borders. It makes you feel like you're a citizen of the planet, not just a citizen of your country."

FUTURE ATTRACTIONS

Where will you go once we can travel even farther into space? Mars is waiting. So are the rings of Saturn and the volcanoes on Io (one of Jupiter's moons). Someday, spaceships will pull alongside asteroids and comets to check them out—the outer-space version of whale-watching! Then there are neighboring galaxies, supernovas, wormholes, maybe even black holes, if you view them from a safe distance.

We can safely say, "The sky's the limit!"

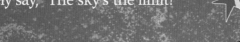

SPACE STORIES

To go places and do things that have never been done before—that's what living is all about.
—ASTRONAUT MICHAEL COLLINS

★ THE LOWDOWN ON GRAVITY, ★ CONTINUED

Ready to understand why gravity is everywhere and yet it seems as if space has no gravity at all?

When the shuttle orbits Earth, two important things are happening. Earth's gravity is pulling the ship back home, so the ship is falling. But it's also in orbit, speeding forward at around 17,500 miles an hour. If the ship went slower, gravity would win and the ship would drop back to Earth. If it sped up, it would break free of Earth's pull. It's the Battle of the Forces—Gravity versus Forward Motion—and it's a tie!

The ship is in what we call free fall. It's falling toward Earth and everything inside is falling along with it. Toothbrushes, guidebooks, even you. If you let go of your hairbrush, it would float right in front of you. That's because you and the hairbrush are both falling at the same speed. If you were floating near the floor and pulled yourself up a foot higher, you'd stay at that new height. That's because the ship and you are both still falling at the same speed.

The result: it feels as if there is no gravity at all. If you leave Earth's orbit, you *still* float around. Wherever you're traveling in your spaceship or space station, you're always orbiting around something—the Moon, the Sun, the Milky Way. The same Battle of the Forces, the same tie, the same microgravity.

★ GLOSSARY ★

cosmonaut: an astronaut of the Russian (formerly known as the Soviet) space program

extraterrestrial: coming from or existing outside Earth's atmosphere

friction: the act of two things rubbing against each other, which slows at least one of them down

galactic cosmic rays: high-energy rays that enter our solar system from other parts of space

geomagnetic storm: a disturbance in our planet's magnetic field caused by high-speed particles ejected by the Sun

g-force: a force against an object that equals the pull of Earth's gravity on that object

lunar: relating to the Moon

Maximum Absorption Garment: the diaper-like garment astronauts wear during liftoff, landing, and space walks, when they can't get to a bathroom

orbit: the path that any object, from a spacecraft to a planet, takes as it revolves around another object

reentry: the act of coming back into Earth's atmosphere after being in space

space junk: objects in orbit around Earth that were created by people but are no longer in use, ranging in size from paint chips to old satellites

space-radiation storm: a storm that occurs when an explosion on the Sun sends out small particles called solar protons, which causes elevated levels of radiation on Earth

space shuttle: a series of US vehicles that carried astronauts and equipment into space on 135 missions from 1981 to 2011

speed of sound: the speed at which sound moves through air, approximately 768 miles an hour; objects going faster than this move at what is called supersonic speed

suborbital flight: a flight without enough altitude or speed to go into orbit

supernova: the final explosion of a star

ultraviolet (UV) rays: light rays emitted by the Sun; invisible to humans, but they burn our skin

wormhole: an imagined or hypothetical shortcut or tunnel that connects two distant points in space and time

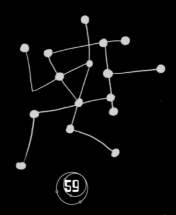

★ SPACE TIME LINE ★

March 16, 1926
Robert H. Goddard launches
the first liquid-fueled rocket.

October 4, 1957
The Soviet Union launches *Sputnik 1*,
the first satellite, into space.

November 3, 1957
The Soviet Union launches
the dog Laika into space on
Sputnik 2. Laika is the first
living being in space.

October 1, 1958
NASA is founded.

April 12, 1961
Russian cosmonaut Yuri Gagarin is the
first human launched into space.

Yuri Gagarin

May 5, 1961
Alan B. Shepard Jr. is the first
American in space.

June 16, 1963
Soviet cosmonaut Valentina Tereshkova is the first woman in space.

March 18, 1965
Soviet cosmonaut Aleksey Leonov makes the first space walk.

July 20, 1969
Traveling to the Moon on *Apollo 11*, Neil Armstrong and Buzz Aldrin are the first humans to step onto the lunar surface.

Buzz Aldrin

April 17, 1970
Apollo 13, which was supposed to land on the Moon, manages to return safely to Earth after a crippling accident and much hardship.

December 14, 1972
Eugene A. Cernan and Harrison H. "Jack" Schmitt of the *Apollo 17* mission are the last people to walk on the Moon's surface.

May 14, 1973
The American space station Skylab is launched. It stays in operation until 1979.

July 15, 1975
Americans and Soviets dock spacecrafts in the first multinational mission.

April 12, 1981
The first US shuttle is launched and is the first reusable spacecraft.

June 18, 1983
Sally Ride is the first American woman in space.

Sally Ride

January 28, 1986
Space shuttle *Challenger* breaks apart seventy-three seconds after liftoff. All seven crew members die, including Christa McAuliffe, who had been picked to become the first teacher in space.

November 20, 1998
The first part of the International Space Station (ISS) is put into orbit.

November 2, 2000
The ISS welcomes its first residents.

April 28, 2001
Blastoff for Dennis Tito, who pays $20 million to become the first tourist in space.

October 4, 2004

Burt Rutan wins the X Prize for *SpaceShipOne*, the first successful privately developed, manned spacecraft.

2005

Virgin Galactic is formed to create a fleet of ships to take private citizens into suborbital space.

December 8, 2010

SpaceX is the first private company to launch a spacecraft into orbit and return it safely to Earth.

SpaceX launch

July 21, 2011

Space shuttle *Atlantis*'s return to Earth officially ends the thirty-year space shuttle program.

May 30, 2012

The US government gives Virgin Galactic permission to begin suborbital test flights of its six-passenger spacecraft.

June 16, 2012

Three Chinese astronauts dock their ship with the first part of the Chinese space station that is planned to be finished in 2020.

October 7, 2012

SpaceX delivers supplies to the International Space Station in its Dragon spacecraft. SpaceX has a contract to take astronauts into space, perhaps as early as 2015.

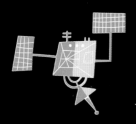

★ FURTHER READING ★
AND SURFING

Just ask any nonfiction writer—research is fun, especially when you have an adventure doing it. Sadly, no one offered me a trip to the ISS to study space firsthand. I did, however, attend Adult Space Academy and a shuttle launch to write two magazine articles. I also spent a week at the kids' version of Space Academy in Huntsville, Alabama, to write a previous children's book.

Yes, I'm an "astro-nut," but I still needed more information for *How Do You Burp in Space?* So I used many grown-up books, including lots of biographies of astronauts to find space slang and the quotations you'll find in this guide. Here are just a few of those books.

Collins, Michael. *Carrying the Fire.* New York: Farrar, Straus and Giroux, 1974.

Comins, Neil F. *The Hazards of Space Travel: A Tourist's Guide.* New York: Villard, 2007.

Harrison, Albert A. *Spacefaring: The Human Dimension.* Berkeley: University of California Press, 2001.

Jones, Tom. *Sky Walking: An Astronaut's Memoir.* New York: HarperCollins, 2006.

Launius, Roger D., and Howard E. McCurdy. *Imagining Space.* San Francisco: Chronicle Books, 2001.

Mullane, Mike. *Riding Rockets: The Outrageous Tales of a Space Shuttle Astronaut.* New York: Scribner, 2006.

The books I used were invaluable, but NASA, the US space agency, is the mother lode of space information. Its website is filled with gorgeous pictures and amazing facts. Even better were all the people there who spoke to me. NASA scientists and technicians know everything under the Sun—over and beyond the Sun as well!

Some of you might think this book is fiction, since serious space tourism has not yet begun. This guide does speculate about a few things, but not very many. Everything from future attractions and menu items to the need for preservation areas on the Moon is based on something that has already happened or is predicted by facts experts already know. Could you really strap on wings and fly in the Moon's gravity? Scientists think so. Do galactic cosmic rays make light shows on your eyelids? Yes, according to Jonathan McDowell of the Harvard-Smithsonian Center for Astrophysics. Will there be solar-storm warnings to keep you from taking a dangerous space walk? Absolutely, says space weather forecaster Larry Combs, who works with NOAA (National Oceanic and Atmospheric Administration) and NASA as well.

Professional authors aren't the only ones who do research. You can, too. If you want to learn more about space travel, start with some of the books below.

Nonfiction Books about Space Travel Past and Present

Aldrin, Buzz. *Look to the Stars.* New York: G. P. Putnam's Sons Books for Young Readers, 2009.

Bingham, Caroline. *First Space Encyclopedia.* New York: DK Publishing, 2008.

Goodman, Susan E. *Ultimate Field Trip 5: Blasting Off to Space Academy.* New York: Atheneum Books for Young Readers, 2001.

Ride, Sally. *To Space and Back.* New York: HarperCollins, 1986.

Thimmesh, Catherine. *Team Moon: How 400,000 People Landed* Apollo 11 *on the Moon.* Boston: Houghton Mifflin Books for Children, 2007.

Nonfiction Books about Future Space Travel

Dyson, Marianne J. *Home on the Moon: Living on a Space Frontier.* Des Moines: National Geographic Children's Books, 2003.

O'Brien, Patrick. *You Are the First Kid on Mars.* New York: G. P. Putnam's Sons Books for Young Readers, 2009.

Novels about Space Travel

Boyce, Bruce Cottrell. *Cosmic.* New York: Walden Pond Press, 2010.

Card, Orson Scott. *Ender's Game.* New York: Tor Science Fiction, 1984.

Daley, Michael. *Shanghaied to the Moon.* New York: G. P. Putnam's Sons Books for Young Readers, 2007.

And the Ultimate Resource

www.nasa.gov

If you want to go to their website especially for kids, with info, videos, and games, try:

www.nasa.gov/audience/forstudents/index.html *and*

www.nasa.gov/audience/forkids/kidsclub/flash/index.html

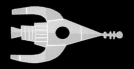

★ QUOTATIONS AND ★
THEIR SOURCES

Page 1: Astronaut Kathryn Thornton, quoted in "Commercial Space Transportation: A Modern Day Everest?" by Dr. George C. Nield. *Ad Astra*, vol. 20, no. 3 (Fall 2008). www.nss.org/adastra/volume20/nield.html

Page 3: Dennis Tito, quoted in "Tito Ralphs in Technicolor." Wired.com, May 1, 2001. www.wired.com/culture/lifestyle/news/2001/05/43460

Page 6: Astronaut Shannon Lucid, quoted in "M&Ms on the Way to Mir to Make Life More Pleasant for Astronaut Lucid," by Seth Borenstein. Orlandosentinel.com, April 12, 1996. http://articles.orlandosentinel.com/1996-04-12/news/9604111175_1_space-station-mir-astronaut-shannon-lucid-atlantis

Page 14: Astronaut Michael P. Anderson, quoted in *Columbia Final Voyage: The Last Flight of NASA's First Space Shuttle*, by Philip Chien; New York: Praxis, 2006.

Page 16: Astronaut Deke Slayton, *Moon Shot: The Inside Story of America's Race to the Moon*, by Alan Shepard and Deke Slayton; Nashville: Turner, 1994.

Page 22: Astronaut Edward White, quoted in "The Glorious Walk in the Cosmos," *Life*, vol. 58, no. 24 (June 18, 1965), p. 39.

Page 24: Astronaut Sunita Williams, quoted in "Space Station Astronaut Ready for Boston Marathon," by Tariq Malik. Space.com, April 4, 2007. www.space.com/3645-space-station-astronaut-ready-boston-marathon.html

Page 27: Astronaut Tom Jones, *Sky Walking: An Astronaut's Memoir*, by Tom Jones; New York: HarperCollins, 2006.

Page 37: Astronaut Sally Ride, *To Space & Back*, by Sally Ride and Susan Okie; New York: HarperCollins, 1989.

Page 45: Astronaut Sultan Bin Salman Bin Abdul Aziz Al-Saud, remarks at I Congress of the Association of Space Explorers. Cernay, France, October 2–6, 1985.

Page 50: Astronaut Alan B. Shepard Jr., quoted on the website of the International Space Hall of Fame at the New Mexico Museum of Space History. www.nmspacemuseum.org/halloffame/detail.php?id=55

Page 51: Astronaut R. Mike Mullane, *Do Your Ears Pop in Space? And 500 Other Surprising Questions about Space Travel*, by R. Mike Mullane; Hoboken, NJ: John Wiley & Sons, 1997.

Page 55: Astronaut Don Thomas, quoted by permission from the astronaut.

Page 55: Astronaut Ken Bowersox, quoted by permission from the astronaut.

Page 56: Astronaut Michael Collins quoted on the website of the International Space Hall of Fame at the New Mexico Museum of Space History. www.nmspacemuseum.org/halloffame/detail.php?id=37

★ ACKNOWLEDGMENTS ★

I owe much to many experts who helped me understand not only space itself and people in space, but also what it would look like to the tourist's eye. A special thanks to astrophysicist Jonathan McDowell at the Chandra X-ray Center of the Harvard-Smithsonian Center for Astrophysics, physicist Michael Horne of Stonehill College, who has been my very eminent physics tutor for years, Larry Combs and William Murtagh of the Space Weather Prediction Center of the National Oceanic and Atmospheric Administration, the countless experts from NASA who graciously explained and fact-checked, plus astronauts Sunita Williams, Don Thomas, and Ken Bowersox who told me about their adventures.

Thanks to Deborah Hirschland and David Elliott for their careful reading and comments. Michael Slack, thanks for adding to the fun with witty, wonderful illustrations. Finally I have heartfelt appreciation for the extraordinary crew at Bloomsbury—especially my space-o-phile buddy Caroline Abbey, Michelle Nagler, Donna Mark, and Beth Eller—who care so much about books every step of the way.

—Susan E. Goodman

★ ABOUT THE AUTHOR ★ AND ILLUSTRATOR

When **SUSAN E. GOODMAN** attended Adult Space Academy in Huntsville, Alabama, she used the same machines astronauts trained on for their missions. She was great at the moonwalk on the one-sixth-gravity chair. After a lengthy session on the Multi-Axis Trainer used by early astronauts to deal with spinning free fall, she couldn't eat for hours. Nevertheless, she'd blast off on the first flight she could. Goodman is also the author of *See How They Run*, *It's a Dog's Life*, and ALA Notable *All in Just One Cookie*. She lives in Massachusetts.

www.susangoodmanbooks.com

When **MICHAEL SLACK** is not creating illustrations for children's books, he can be found in his microgravity chamber developing space burping techniques and practicing eating upside down. Slack is also the illustrator of *Scapegoat*, *My Life as a Chicken*, and *Pizza, Pigs, and Poetry*. He lives in California.

www.slackart.com

★ INDEX ★